From Tow Truck to Auto Body Shop

Meg Greve

rourkeeducationalmedia.com

Scan for Related Titles and Teacher Resources

Teaching Focus:
Fluency: Using Expression- Have students read aloud to practice reading with expression and with appropriate pacing.

Before Reading:

Building Academic Vocabulary and Background Knowledge
Before reading a book, it is important to set the stage for your child or students by using pre-reading strategies. This will help them develop their vocabulary, increase their reading comprehension, and make connections across the curriculum.

1. *Read the title and look at the cover. Let's make predictions about what this book will be about.*
2. *Take a picture walk by talking about the pictures/photographs in the book. Implant the vocabulary as you take the picture walk. Be sure to talk about the text features such as headings, Table of Contents, glossary, bolded words, captions, charts/ diagrams, or Index.*
3. Have students read the first page of text with you then have students read the remaining text.
4. *Strategy Talk – use to assist students while reading.*
   - *Get your mouth ready*
   - *Look at the picture*
   - *Think…does it make sense*
   - *Think…does it look right*
   - *Think…does it sound right*
   - *Chunk it – by looking for a part you know*
5. *Read it again.*
6. *After reading the book complete the activities below.*

Content Area Vocabulary
Use glossary words in a sentence.

assistance
auto
community
employees
transportation
vehicle

After Reading:

Comprehension and Extension Activity
After reading the book, work on the following questions with your child or students in order to check their level of reading comprehension and content mastery.

1. *What are some things a mechanic can fix on a car?* (Asking questions)
2. *Why would someone call a tow truck?* (Summarize)
3. *Have you ever been in a mechanic's shop? Tell us about it.* (Text to self connection)
4. *How do tow truck drivers and mechanics work together?* (Asking questions)

Extension Activity
Look around your community! Usually there are several auto body or mechanic shops in each city or town. When you are on the bus or in the car going home, look out the window and count how many auto body or mechanic shops you pass. How many did you see? Were they located all over town or just in one spot? Why is it important to have several in each town? Which one is closest to your house?

jkjc

Transportation is important in any **community**. Cars take kids to and from school, trucks deliver goods to stores, and buses move people from place to place.

3

But what happens if your transportation stops working?

Job Shop

Cars breakdown for lots of reasons. You might run out of gas, get a flat tire, or get in an accident.

There are many people in the community who can help you solve your transportation troubles.

Tow truck operators, mechanics, gas stations, and **auto** body shops are people and places to use when your **vehicle** stops working.

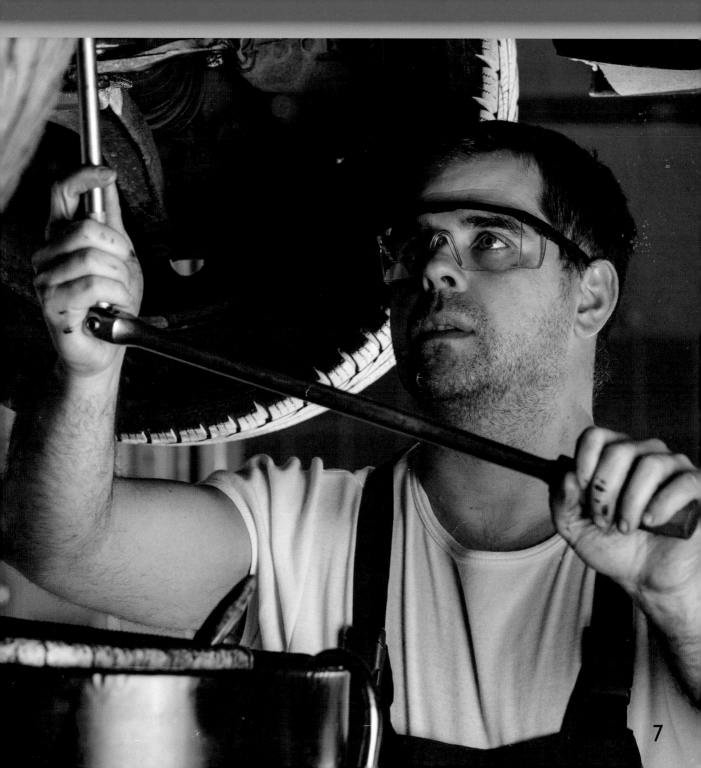

If the car has a flat tire or runs out of gas, someone who works for a roadside **assistance** program will come right to the car and fix it.

Job Shop

People who work for these programs are usually mechanics trained to fix cars.

9

When a car cannot move anymore, some people call a tow truck. The tow truck driver uses special equipment on a truck to lift the car and pull it on its back wheels or carry it.

Types of Tow Trucks

Light Duty Tow Truck

Car Carrier

Job-Shop

Other names for a tow truck are wreckers, breakdown trucks, and draggin' wagons.

Heavy Duty Tow Truck

Tow truck drivers use special equipment on the back of their trucks to load and pull cars and trucks.

Tow truck drivers have to get special training in order to drive a tow truck and tow a vehicle.

Once the vehicle arrives at the auto body shop, a mechanic will work to find the problem and fix it.

Job Shop

Mechanics are often called automotive service technicians. They work in many places including car dealerships, service stations, gas stations, and even some police stations!

15

Mechanics use many tools, such as jacks, screwdrivers, wrenches, and even computers. They are good problem-solvers too.

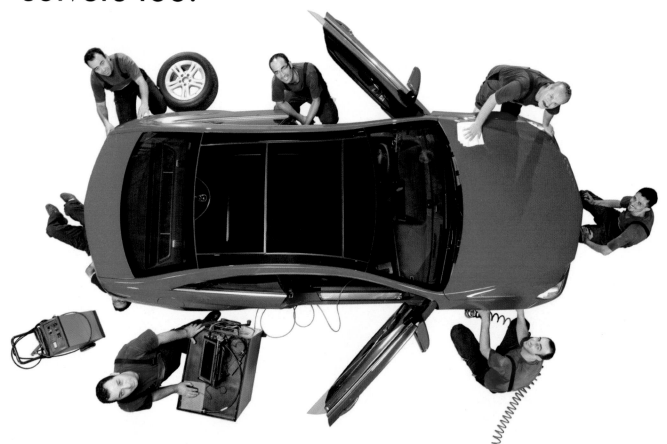

Tools of the Trade

Hand Winch

Creeper

Wrench

Socket Set

Scissor Jack

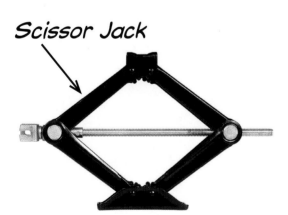

Some mechanics work on their own, and others work in shops owned by other people.

Where Do You Get Your Car Fixed?

Body Shop

Oil Change Shop

Service Station

Tire Shop

Shop owners are usually mechanics too. They work with the customers, buy parts for the shop, and hire their **employees**.

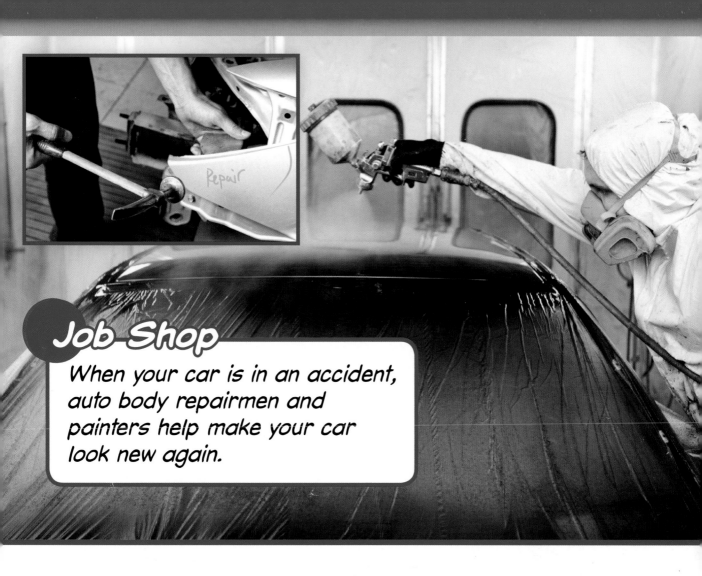

Job Shop

When your car is in an accident, auto body repairmen and painters help make your car look new again.

These jobs might be for you if you like cars, fixing problems, and working with your hands!

Photo Glossary

 **assistance** (uh-SISS-tuhnss): Help with a problem.

 **auto** (AW-toh): Short for automobile, a car.

 **community** (kuh-MYOO-nuh-tee): A group of people who live and work near one another.

 **employees** (em-PLOI-ees): People who work for other people.

 **transportation** (transs-pur-TAY-shuhn): A of way moving people from one place to another, such as in a car, truck, bus, train, or airplane.

 **vehicle** (VEE-uh-kuhl): Something that can be used to move people or other things from one place to another.

Index

Websites to Visit

www.sciencekids.co.nz/sciencefacts/vehicles/cars.html
wonderopolis.org/wonder/why-do-you-change-the-oil-in-cars
www.wikihow.com/Change-a-Tire

About the Author

Meg Greve lives in Chicago with her husband Tom, and her two children, Madison and William. She usually takes her car to a shop even though her dad taught her how to change a tire and change the oil!

Meet The Author!
www.meetREMauthors.com

© 2015 Rourke Educational Media

www.rourkeeducationalmedia.com

PHOTO CREDITS: Cover © DarrenMower, loraks; title page © Terry Wilson; page 3 © Blend Images/Ariel Skelley; page 4 © Rusian Dashinsky; page 5 © Wendy Townrow, Jason Lugo; page 6 © Andresr; page 7 © Zorandim; page 8 © michaeljung; page 9 © Monkia Wisniewska; page 10 © Mert Toker; page 11 © Joe_Potato, Mikadun, TFoxFoto; page 12 © Olinchuk; page 13 © Eliza Snow-Lightstyle Photography; page 14 © Kali Nine LLC; page 15 © Minerva Studio; page 16 © 1001nights page 17 © Yanas; page 18 © XiXinXing; page 19 © loraks, Slobo Mitic, runzelkorn; page 20 © aydinmutiu; page 21 © Krzyssztof Reczek, Diane Labombarbe

Edited by: Luana Mitten
Cover design by: Jen Thomas
Interior design by: Rhea Magaro

Library of Congress PCN Data

From Tow Truck to Auto Body Shop/ Meg Greve
(Little World Communities and Commerce)
ISBN (hard cover)(alk. paper) 978-1-63430-062-9
ISBN (soft cover) 978-1-63430-092-6
ISBN (e-Book) 978-1-63430-119-0
Library of Congress Control Number: 2014953342
Printed in the United States of America, North Mankato, Minnesota

Also Available as:

ROURKE'S
e-Books